Dog Daycare: A Supervisor's Training Guide

Nikki Ivey

Copyright © 2014 Nikki Ivey

All rights reserved.

ISBN:1495276503
ISBN-13:9781495276507

DEDICATION

This book is dedicated to all those dog lovers who have chosen to educate themselves on developing dogs to their full potential. May the information in this book give you the skills you need to be successful in your job.

CONTENTS

ACKNOWLEDGMENTS

I want to thank Britteny Watson for all of her hard work on editing this book. You are not only the best partner one could have but your talent in marketing, public relations and editing surpass everything I could have hoped for. I want to thank God for the gift He has given me in working with dogs. I'm blessed every day that I get to share my knowledge with dog owners and professional alike.

Introduction

Congratulations on your decision to become a Dog Daycare Supervisor. This book goes with the online Dog Daycare Supervisor Certification Course available at E-Training For Dogs. If you are not enrolled in this course you can still benefit from reading and studying the information in this book. If you choose to take the course you may do so at www.e-trainingfordogs.com. The course will give you a much more in-depth look at dog behavior, communication and interaction. It is packed full of videos of dogs interacting which will give you more understanding than just reading the book. Reading alone will not give you the education you need to become a certified dog daycare supervisor. However, reading this book is a great start to that goal.

I hope you enjoy the book as much as I did writing it. When you complete this book you will have more knowledge than the average dog daycare supervisor. You will be ready to move on to the next level of dog daycare supervision. You will be prepared to gain experience and further your knowledge. The more knowledge you have, the more you will help the dogs in your care.

Chapter 1
Importance of Dog Daycare and Supervisor Training

What is Dog Daycare?

Dog daycare is a service that allows dogs to interact under the supervision of humans. Daycare is a great way to allow dogs to burn off extra energy, improve confidence and learn how to properly interact with other dogs. Most daycares in the US, however, focus primarily on play and the expenditure of energy. It is important that daycares focus on teaching good habits and real life manners to the dogs in their care. A great daycare will not only physically stimulate a dog, it will also mentally stimulate it.

Daycare allows dogs to interact with other dogs of different sizes, play styles, temperaments, and confidence and communication levels. By learning how to interact with dogs with different personalities, a dog is more capable of handling stress or changes in its environment. Dogs are born with innate signals that help them communicate their emotions to other dogs and people. We call these signals calming signals, also known as dog or body language. Dogs communicate solely with their bodies, which is why they can read humans so easily. The purpose of these signals is to avoid conflict, to calm a situation or to calm themselves. Dogs must be experienced in using these signals if they want to have the ability to handle stressors.

Though dogs are born with the natural ability to use dog language, they must continue practicing these signals to be confident when using them. If they are unable to practice using it due to a lack of socialization, they tend to lose the ability to handle stress and their confidence drops dramatically. This typically results in the dog developing fears and phobias.

Daycare is a wonderful opportunity for dogs to use their dog language skills, build confidence and to learn self-control. Laying this foundation can prevent behavior issues that may be difficult to correct later. Many dogs with behavioral issues are relinquished to shelters or rescues. Most behavior problems can be avoided if the dog is properly socialized and owners are properly educated on the importance of understanding dog language. This is where you, the daycare supervisor or employee, can play a profound role in a dog's life.

Though not every dog that comes into your daycare facility will have bad dog language skills or behavioral issues, each will need you to reinforce and reward proper behavior. As a daycare supervisor, it is imperative that you understand how and why dogs communicate. The only way a daycare can be successful in assisting dogs to become better with their language skills is through staff training and practice. Daycares are oftentimes unsuccessful due to bad publicity or lawsuits related to injuries or illnesses of clients' dogs. You will find that through staff training, many injuries can be avoided.

Ask yourself the following questions to determine if your daycare is on the right path to becoming or staying successful:

1. **What is your percentage of new dog evaluations vs. the percentage of the dogs that pass?**

    In order to appropriately evaluate a new dog coming into your facility you must first understand dog personality, dog language and dog interaction. A proper evaluation will tell you about how a dog plays and interacts with others, as well as what issues may arise when he joins a group. Successful daycares will do evaluations throughout the week. Approximately 99% of dogs will, and should, pass evaluations and be allowed to use your facility.

2. **Do you ban particular breeds in daycare?**

    There are many daycares that ban certain breeds. By doing this, daycare owners are missing out on potential income. They also inhibit these dogs from learning valuable skills they need in order to communicate with humans and other dogs. There are instances where local laws prohibit certain breeds from being in a city. Keep in mind that the breed of dog does not necessarily determine the personality of the dog. While some bully breeds may be more predisposed to stubbornness, they will not always be bullies or cause problems in your facility. This is why staff training and proper evaluations are imperative for a daycare business.

3. **Do you believe that if a dog does not play perfectly in daycare with every dog daycare is not right for him?**

    Daycare is not just for young, well-behaved, small or energetic dogs. While some dogs may require extra training prior to entering a daycare group, there are very few dogs who are truly unsuitable for daycare. Puppies and young dogs are great for daycare when they are mixed with adult dogs. Patient adult dogs with good skills and signals will assist young and other inexperienced dogs with building self-control, confidence and dog language skills.

Senior dogs are often left out of playgroups. Many believe that because seniors do not play that it is a waste of money to have them attend. In reality, daycare can provide older dogs with much needed socialization and exercise, which will help with their overall wellbeing and health. This keeps their joints and muscles moving which helps prevent stiffness. Older dogs are also great teachers for dogs that think everyone wants to play. Many senior dogs have the confidence to assist with teaching younger dogs proper signals without going "overboard."

Dogs with severe fear issues will require training before attending daycare. In these cases, I recommend confidence building training for a couple of weeks before daycare is attempted. I never recommend keeping a severely fearful dog out of daycare for the entirety of its life, as learning to use dog language on a regular basis will help to build confidence, which will alleviate some of the fear. Dogs that do not play well should also not be left out of daycare. They may need some self-control training before attending daycare but they should have the opportunity to improve their play. They may be required to play with a special group until they are able to be integrated with the normal pack.

Dogs with severe health issues may need to be removed from daycare depending on the nature of the condition and recommendation of the dog's veterinarian. I have found some large dogs with hip issues, however, may still be able to attend daycare if put with the proper group. I will often mix him with smaller dogs so he can still interact with other dogs without the fear of having others jump on his back or hips. Dogs that attack other dogs with no warning (this means no sniffing or posturing first) should not be in daycare. It is very rare you will meet a dog with true dog aggression. Dogs that have aggression towards humans should also be left out of daycare. If a supervisor is unable to have a relationship with a dog it will make it difficult to establish leadership and interrupt inappropriate behavior. Again, it is rare that a dog can be deemed truly vicious or aggressive. It is important that these dogs be thoroughly evaluated by a behavioral consultant prior to daycare.

Again, 99% of dogs evaluated for daycare should pass their evaluations. They may need a special playgroup or extra attention, but they should be able to get the same benefits from daycare as other regular attendees.

4. **Do you have more than three fights a week? Are regular dogs beginning to cause problems in group? Are you**

unable to take in new clients because you feel overwhelmed with the regular group attending?

Unfortunately, many facilities attempt to operate daycares without appropriately trained staff. This can cause serious injury to the dogs in their care as well as to their staff. There is a lot of knowledge that daycare supervisors and staff must have in order to be successful and safe.

All supervisors and staff participating in daycare should have an understanding of dog communication. Dog communication is how dogs avoid conflict, express their emotions and calm themselves. This will be discussed in depth in a later chapter. When supervisors do not understand dog communication they are unable to clearly read the signals dogs offer in daycare. This can cause an increase in potentially dangerous altercations. This will also ensure staff is safe during dog evaluations and while in a play area with a large group of dogs.

Staff should also have an understanding of how dogs play and interact. Understanding how dogs interact and play will allow staff to know when and how to appropriately interrupt inappropriate play, and when play should be allowed to continue.

Many people believe that getting to work with dogs all day is the ultimate job and in a way, it is. However, it is not as luxurious as many may think. Working with dogs in a daycare setting is a demanding job that requires considerable education, patience and confidence.

A successful daycare supervisor is one that is looking for a career, and not just a job. As an owner, look for someone who is interested in changing the lives of dogs as well as someone who wants to and can build your business. A successful daycare supervisor must also be responsible, mature and driven. Ensure that the potential supervisor is not easily distracted, and is able to remain calm in potentially stressful situations. A supervisor should always be willing to learn new things related to dog behavior and interaction.

Finally, a supervisor must have great communication skills, both verbally and written as they will be expected to keep records, write evaluations and speak to clients on behalf of the business.

Chapter 2
Supervisors' Roles & Responsibilities

Supervising Daycare

It is important that a supervisor understand his/her role when it comes to daycare. The supervisor is the most important person within the pack. As a supervisor, you must be able to:

- Be the leader
- Control the environment; the gate
- Control the dogs
- Keep the area clean
- Keep water bowls cleaned and filled
- Evaluate all dogs for daycare
- Fill out evaluation forms and report cards
- Explain dog behavior to clients (minimally)
- Sell daycare to clients

When you are out in the yard with the daycare group, there are some do's and don'ts that need to be followed to ensure a harmonious time for all.

Do:

- Stop bad behavior before it occurs
- Know your dogs
- Reward good behavior by acknowledging verbally

- Stay calm
- Be the leader
- Practice your skills
- Be in control
- Allow dogs to be dogs
- Ignore dogs that jump on you
- Keep yard clean
- Water bowls clean and filled
- Improve dog's behavior
- Continually evaluate dogs
- Limit interaction (play, petting) with dogs

Don't:

- Allow dogs in lap
- Baby or coddle nervous or fearful dogs
- Play tug
- Play fetch with a large group or with any dogs that have resource issues or that reach the heightened state of arousal quickly
- Be overly attentive to dogs by petting and playing
- Interrupt good play
- Be distracted
- Acknowledge behavior like jumping, barking at you, pushing toys into your face or lap, nudging you or pawing at you
- Allow dogs to disrespect signals

- Play using a water hose as a toy
- Use physical corrections
- Use spray bottles for correction
- Use a loud voice by screaming at the dogs
- Use a deep, firm voice when interacting with the dogs
- Stand in the middle of the pack

Multiple Supervisors

Many facilities have multiple supervisors. This can be beneficial for new or inexperienced supervisors or for days when there are multiple or more rambunctious group. Having multiple supervisors also allows businesses to offer more days of daycare without employee burnout, or to have a backup plan in case an employee must be out of work. There are certain rules to apply in the case of having multiple supervisors at a facility. Each supervisor should have the same knowledge and education. This will ensure that each supervisor is acknowledging dogs for appropriate behavior, and is properly interrupting inappropriate behavior consistently.

Each supervisor must also know what their role is during each shift. One supervisor may be in charge of clean-up while the other supervisor is in charge of keeping play safe. Both supervisors may agree to do both jobs together. If this is the case, it is important that follow-through occurs. If one supervisor begins to interrupt a particular dog, that supervisor must follow through by taking the appropriate steps to interrupt the behavior. The supervisor will then be responsible for interrupting this same dog if he repeats the behavior within a five minute period. If the dog ends up in a time-out, the supervisor that put the dog in must release it from the time-out. Once out of time-out, the slate is clean and either supervisor can interrupt the dog for inappropriate behavior.

Chapter 3
Dog Communication in Daycare

Dog language is the utilization of specific body postures, noises and actions that help a dog to communicate effectively with other dogs and people. A dog's sole purpose for using dog language is to avoid conflict. Dogs perceive conflict differently than humans. Dog conflict may be perceived when another dog or human plays too rough, when a human, animal or object approaches too quickly, or when a human is loud or overly confrontational. Conflict can also be caused by elements in the environment such as thunder, fireworks, cameras or cars. Avoiding conflict does not always mean a dog is trying to thwart a fight, it means he is trying to pacify himself and/or what makes him uncomfortable. Dogs need to learn how to appropriately communicate with other dogs and conversely, humans need to know how to read this language.

Dog language is an important part of dog daycare. Dogs spend all day interacting and communicating. As a supervisor, you must understand communication signals in order to keep interaction appropriate and respectful. Knowing communication signals will allow you to evaluate dogs and communicate clearly with them your expectations.

Calming Signals

There are **three levels of calming signals dogs use in order to communicate**. These levels range from passive (Level 1) to aggressive (Level 3). Dog language can be difficult to detect and decipher until you are introduced to it. After which, it becomes obvious and even entertaining.

Dogs offer a *behavior* when they want something, like a treat, a toy, or play. They offer a *signal* when they want to solicit a calming effect.

Level 1 – Passive Signals

Level 1 is the most innate level of signals used, *only if* the dog has had a chance to practice dog language. Many dogs lack proficient communication skills because they do not get adequate interaction with other dogs. Although born with the ability to communicate, dogs must practice these skills on a regular basis. If not, they lack the confidence to control a situation that may escalate into conflict. Dogs with insufficient language skills usually skip Level 1 signals.

Head Turn:

This is the most commonly used signal. A dog will slowly turn his head from side to side, avoiding eye contact. He may do this for many seconds before attempting another signal in order to give the conflict a chance to appropriately diminish. You probably see this signal often when trying to photograph a dog because many dogs see cameras as a conflict. You can use this signal to calm a dog that is nervous, shy or overly excited.

Body Turn:

A dog will turn his entire body from a frontal position and show you his side or he may turn all the way around and show you his rear. This is another great signal that you can use to help calm down a dog. This is the most effective technique when dealing with a jumping dog.

Eye Aversion:

This is when a dog will avert his eyes away from you without necessarily turning his head or body. You will often see dogs do this when you have a dog's face in your hands, and he cannot turn his head.

Sit:

Dogs will sit when dealing with a new dog, an overly excited dog or a human who is being too forceful. Many times a sit will become a default behavior when a dog does not know what else to do to appease a situation. To understand if the action is a signal or a behavior, look at the rest of the body. If it is used as a signal, the dog will use it with another signal like turning the head or averting the eyes. If it is a behavior, the dog will sit and look towards the other dog or human. This is a great signal to use when dealing with nervous or shy dogs. Instead of sitting, I recommend squatting so it is easier to move away or closer to the dog depending on the response he is giving you. When you squat, you will always use another signal like head turning, body turning or averting the eyes.

Down:

This signal is not as common as the previous. Little dogs are more likely to use the down as a signal or behavior than a larger dog. Dogs with a high level of confidence will also be more likely to use this signal. Like a sit, you will see other behaviors combined with it. Always look at the rest of the body and in what context the down is being used.

Bow:

This can be used as a signal or as a behavior. When used as a signal, a dog will go into the bow position where his front legs are stretched out in front and his bottom is up in the air. However, unlike a play bow where a dog will jump from side-to-side quickly as a play invitation, a dog will remain stationary when using a bow as a calming signal. When it is a signal, you will often times see it mixed with another signal like averting eyes or turning the head. Dogs that have very good dog skills will sometimes use a bow as a signal and behavior at the same time. He may want another dog to play, but if the other dog is anxious, the bowing dog may offer a calming signal to relieve the tension of the encounter. You can use this as a signal yourself, but you may feel silly doing it. I recommend using the more natural signals like head and body turns, eye aversion and sitting/squatting.

Quick Licks:

This signal is difficult to see until you are used to spotting it. A quick lick is when the tongue comes out of the mouth and in a very quick motion licks the nose and then quickly moves back in. A dog that uses this will do it several times in a row to try and get his point across. Quick licks will also be combined with other signals.

Raised Paw:

This signal is not used as often as the others. When a dog is using this as a signal, he will slightly raise the paw and use another signal with it. Keep in mind you must read the entire body in order to identify this as a calming signal. If the dog is a pointer, for instance, a raised paw may mean the dog is simply pointing something.

Doing Something Else (Ignoring):

A dog will do this when he wants to extinguish a behavior. He may sniff the ground, urinate and/or completely ignore what it is he wants to extinguish. Many people see this as a dog being stubborn but in most cases, the dog is trying to calm a situation. For example, your dog, Jake, is playing in the yard and you call him to you. He does not listen to you the first three times. Why? He may not know the command. Or, if he does, you could be using a harsh tone that he views as a conflict. If the latter is correct, Jake will ignore you and wait for you to calm down.

Yawning:

Dogs yawn for two reasons. He may yawn because he is tired or as a signal to calm a situation or himself. Look at what context the yawn is being used to help you decide if it is a signal or a behavior. On occasion, a dog will use this with other signals.

Curving:

When meeting a new dog or sometimes, a new person, a dog will curve towards the object to show calmness and friendliness. This is where dogs will greet one another by smelling their rear ends or genitalia. This seems rude to us, but in reality, meeting face-to-face is inappropriate and confrontational in a dog's world. Many dogs, especially puppies, are not good at this signal due to a lack of experience and maturity. Poor greeting signals will often start a scuffle. Use this method when meeting a new dog. Walking up to the dog from the side, and curving to greet him. Do not approach a strange dog from the front. And I suggest that you never bend over a dog that you are unfamiliar with its personality.

Splitting Up:

If you have ever had a dog sit or stand between you and another person, (i.e. while cuddling on the couch with your significant other), you have probably seen this signal. Many people think this is a cute gesture of jealousy, however the dog actually sees this as a conflict and is trying to *literally* split you apart. During play, dogs will do this when they sense other dogs' rough play will cause a fight. Confident, experienced dogs will walk between two dogs, and will stay with the offending dog until it redirects, much like an umpire during a sporting match. This signal takes a lot of practice as most dogs lack the consistency, confidence and follow-through to do it properly. The more a dog has a chance to interact with other dogs, the better he will become.

Level 2 - Less Passive Signals

Level 2 signals are less passive and very easily recognized. Many humans become uncomfortable when they see Level 2 signals, often labeling a dog as vicious. Dogs will use Level 2 signals if they do not have confidence, time to use Level 1 signals, or to articulate to the other dog that his patience is growing thin.

Growling:

A dog will give a low growl to let another dog or person know he is uncomfortable. This means that the dog is *trying* to control a potentially conflicting situation. When growling is used as a signal it is mixed with other signals such as a head turn. If growling is a behavior, other signals are not used, and the dog's posture will be stiff and he will stare at the person or dog ahead of him. If you have a patient dog with good dog language, he will often try Level 1 signals first. If using Level 1 signals is not effective, he will be forced to escalate to Level 2. For example, if a family pet is constantly harassed by a child at home, (say the child is crawling all over him, chasing him down, getting in his face, etc.), and the dog's Level 1 signals are being ignored, the dog will be forced to escalate to Level 2. When the dog growls at the child, the family scolds the dog instead of educating the child, or they improperly assume the dog is vicious, and re-home the dog or worse. This scenario is one that occurs all too often. It is important to know whether the dog had previously displayed Level 1 signals prior to the growl, and before jumping to Level 2.

Snarling:

A snarl occurs when a dog pulls his lips up and shows his teeth. This signal is often used with a low growl and always with a Level 1 signal such as a quick lick, head turn or eye aversion. Many fearful dogs with no confidence will resort to this behavior immediately when faced with an uncomfortable situation. Dogs with confidence will use a snarl if they do not have time to use a Level 1 signal, (i.e. when another dog is suddenly in his face). Like the growl, if it is not mixed with other signals, it is being given as a behavior with the possibility of turning into aggression.

Level 3 – Aggressive Signals

Level 3 is considered the Aggressive Level. When a dog uses Level 3 signals, it does not mean he is vicious or is an aggressive dog, it just means that the signals are much more noticeable to the untrained eye. Dogs use this Level when Levels 1 and 2 did not work or he does not have the patience or skills to do Levels 1 and 2 first. Level 3 signals are very obvious and often make people nervous. Because of their lack of understanding, they will often punish or correct a dog for offering Level 3 signals. This will normally make the dog resort to level 3 faster than usual, because of the association of correction or punishment when another dog gets too close. Level 3 signals can also be behaviors from a dog that is being a bully so you must read the dog's entire body to understand.

Muzzle Grab:

A muzzle grab occurs when a dog attempts to place his mouth over another dog's muzzle. This may be a sign of dominance because it places another dog into a submissive position. Humans sometimes use a version of this by purchasing head halters that go over the muzzle of their dog. This is placed into the aggressive level, because there is physical contact between the dogs. Though the dog giving signals does not intend to cause harm, the dog receiving the muzzle grab will oftentimes get a cut on the bridge of the muzzle because the skin is thin in this area. This behavior is acceptable when the previous two levels have not worked. Most young puppies experience this at least once in their life. If you observe a dog is not respecting Level 1 and 2 signals, you should correct the disrespectful dog—not the dog giving the signals.

Snapping:

When giving this signal a dog will snap towards whatever needs calming, and then back away quickly. This occurs when humans who do not understand that the dog has been displaying Level 1 and 2 signals and continue to place the dog in an uncomfortable and stressful environment. When the conflict is not resolved, then the dog will escalate to snapping. A dog at this level is usually snapping out of fear, or lacks the confidence and maturity to disengage emotionally from what is causing the fear. Essentially, all he wants is to avoid conflict and to make something go away. The dog that uses snapping as a behavior, will often not back down after snapping. This is the difference between a dog using proper dog language or getting caught up in his fear turning dangerously aggressive. This is also the number one signal that is used when a dog has no confidence or does not understand the first two levels.

Biting:

Often times biting is a dog's last resort when other signals have not worked. Like a dog that uses a snap, dogs with low confidence or language skills often bite instead of offering Level 1 or 2 signals. If a dog is using this as a signal, the dog will often bite and then back off. I define a bite as a snap with contact. A signal bite is different than a warning bite. A dog that is using the bite as a warning behavior will hold and shake its victim and not back down. A hold and shake will cause more damage than a signal bite and release.

When observing any Level 3 signals, you must not jump to conclusions. Level 3 signals do not necessarily mean that the dog is vicious and cannot be rehabilitated. You must evaluate the dog carefully to adequately evaluate why the dog used this level of signals or behavior. Is he offering Level 1 and 2 first or is he going immediately to Level 3? The more you observe, the more competent you will be at evaluating the dog.

Various Signals

Dogs give other dogs and humans various signals that help them communicate. These signals are not necessarily calming signals, and are typically easy to recognize.

Tail Wag:

This is the most misunderstood signal. A tail wag does not always mean "happy dog". A tail wag means a dog is aroused in one form or another. When evaluating what a particular tail wag means look at the entire body for confirmation. Also, take a dog's breed into consideration. Many dogs do not have tails, and others normally have a stiff or curled tail.

If a dog's tail is **slow and relaxed**, the dog is comfortable in the current situation. I also refer to this as the "flag" wag, because it often looks like a flag blowing in the wind.

A **high, stiff and slow wag** means the dog is being challenging or taking a defensive posture. If it is not moving, the dog could be trying to calm another dog. I refer to this wag as a "stick in low wind."

A **high, stiff and fast wag** means a dog is highly aroused.

Arousal can come from a variety of sources. This is also known as the "stick in a hurricane" wag.

A fast to moderate and relaxed wags means a dog is happy and comfortable. Often times the wag will make a circle, which is why I refer to this as a "circle wag."

If a dog has a **low/no wag,** the dog is uncomfortable from fear or nervousness. A low/no wag can also come from pain. Sometimes the tail will be tucked between the legs.

Raised Hackles:

At some point you will see the fur on the back or neck of a dog stand up. This is a natural response to arousal. Arousal can be from excitement, being unsure, low confidence, and/or aggression. A dog that has his hackles raised is not necessarily getting ready to attack. You must always read the entire body of a dog to really understand what he is trying to communicate. Again, you must be aware of the breed. Breeds such as Rhodesian ridgebacks have raised fur all the time.

Shake Off:

Shake offs are used as a "release" which can denote the beginning of play or the end of a sequence of events, (i.e. after a long introduction, a dog shakes off to show he is ready for play).

Barking:

Dog use barking as a vocal way to communicate. Keep in mind a mastiff and a Chihuahua will have different low-pitched barks:

A **high-pitched bark** indicates excitement, heavy arousal, fearfulness or nervousness.

A **low-pitched bark** is used for warning or frustration.

Distance Increasing Signals

These signals are used to increase the distance between a dog and a conflict. When a dog is uncomfortable with something (i.e. another dog that is too close), he will use these signals as a way to express his desire to be away from the conflict.

Whining, Yelping and Crying:

These will often come from insecure puppies or dogs that are unable to use calming signals properly. Crying and whining is a vocal way of demonstrating frustration and not used for distance increasing. Yelping can be associated with pain, (think about the last time you accidentally stepped on your dog's tail).

Humans Can Speak Dog

Humans are capable of communicating with dogs by using these same signals. Whether you have a dog that is afraid, nervous or outgoing, you can calm him by using these same signals. Practice using these signals with your own dog until they become second nature to you. Start by seeing how well your dog responds to them. How well they respond will tell you how well they know dog language, as well as help you improve your own skills. **Use only Level 1 signals** with dogs and be sure to be confident and consistent!

A **head turn** is easy to use with a jumping or nervous dog. Be sure to completely ignore the dog (no touching or talking) while using this signal.

A **body turn** is a great way to deal with a jumping dog. When the dog sits for 3-5 seconds, verbally acknowledge the dog for being good. If the dog jumps again, turn your body and ignore him. If the dog is causing you pain from jumping, ignore the dog and walk to another room.

Use a **sit or squat** with a nervous or fearful dog (if they are not oversized.) Always keep your body turned to the side.

In order for **yawning** to work, you must be consistent. Mix this with another signal such as a head turn. You can use this signal to your advantage when dealing with a nervous or shy dog. For instance, if a dog is afraid of thunderstorms, make sure the dog is near you. Simply ignore the dog (do not coddle), and yawn from time to time. You may see the dog begin to yawn back. He is trying to calm himself.

Again, **curving** should always be used when meeting a new dog. Approach the dog from the side, and curve to greet. Do not approach a dog head on.

Split-ups should not be overused. It is essential that you are confident and consistent when walking in between two dogs. Follow-though is crucial in order for this signal to work. For example, if your dog is barking at a door, confidently position yourself between the dog and the door. Move your body toward the dog until it redirects. Do not talk or touch the dog. If the dog gets around you and returns to the door, do not panic. Simply start over.

Chapter 4
Understanding Dog Interaction

Dogs must interact in order to learn the proper dog skills to help them avoid conflict. Misunderstanding dog interaction can be detrimental to the success of a dog daycare. By not understanding appropriate behavior, many supervisors interrupt dogs too often. This can lead to frustrated dogs, and can also promote behavior issues such as a lack of self-control, dog aggression, fear or anxiety. Dogs initially learn how to interact with their mother and littermates in order to get their needs met. As the pups grow they continue learning about interaction through play. Play occurs between the littermates and the mother. After leaving the litter, they continue learning by playing with friends or siblings. A puppy should have the opportunity to play with many different types of dogs, each varying in personality, age and size. This will help the puppy learn the difference between appropriate and inappropriate play and signals.

As a supervisor you will have the ability to help dogs improve the way they interact with one another, therefore improving their communication skills.

Types of Interaction

There are three different types of interactions that occur between dogs:

1. Greetings

There are two steps to the greeting process. The first is the approach. During the initial approach dogs should begin communicating by curving, and turning their heads and bodies. They should approach slowly, allowing the other dog to receive, respect and respond to the signals given. By approaching appropriately the dogs have a higher chance of getting along. If a dog approaches incorrectly, (by running straight up to another dog), a negative first impression could be made, and an altercation could occur. Many dogs have a difficult time with this process due to a lack of communication skills and self-control.

The second step in the greeting process is the introduction. The introduction begins when the dogs get within touching distance of one another. Their bodies should remain in a curved fashion. They will then approach each other on the backside for a sniff. This is how they get to know each other. This process should occur with the initial greeting only and does not have to be repeated if the dogs know each other. Once this step is completed, the greeting is over and the next step in interaction can begin. As a supervisor, you should praise appropriate skills during the both steps of the greeting process.

2. Play

Dogs initiate play in seven different ways. Some of these may be combined to increase the chances that he will get a positive response.

1. **Lying on Back:** Dogs will often times roll over to expose their bellies when initiating play. The purpose is not to bow down to the other dog but to show a submissive attitude. By doing this, the dog initiating is hoping to relax the receiving dog enough to get play started.

2. **Offering A Toy:** Dogs use toys on a regular basis to offer play-both with humans and dogs. They may put the toy in the face of another dog to tempt him to play tug. They will also play keep-a-way to in order to initiate a game of chase.

3. **Nudging:** This is where a dog will take his nose and poke the other dog. They will typically poke along the neck and shoulder area. This nudging action is considered rude if the other dog is ignoring or offering other calming signals, and the dog initiating play ignores these signals or nudges harder. In these instances, you will interrupt the dog who is being rude.

4. **Paw Tap:** A paw tap is used similar to nudging except the dog will use his paw. Your own dog may do this to you at home while you are sitting on the couch, and he hopes to gain your attention. Just as with nudging, if the dog offering this behavior does not respect the signals of a dog who does not want to play, you must interrupt.

5. **Play Bow:** This is the most common and recognizable initiation of play. This occurs when a dog stretches his front feet out and has his rear in the air. This differs from a calming bow or just a stretch in that he will also be bouncing from side to side in front of the dog with whom he wants to play.

6. **Barking:** This initiation will often be mixed with the other offers of play, such as the play bow. This behavior can become excessive and disrespectful if the other dog is trying to ignore or walk away from him.

7. **Whining:** Similar to barking, this behavior will be mixed with other offers to play.

Play Styles:

Once play has been initiated, dogs will play in one of four play <u>styles:</u>

1. **Wrestling:** Two or three dogs will be often times stationary with one on the bottom and the other two bouncing around and playing on top. This can be mixed with the chase game as well. Wrestling is the type of play that is often misunderstood by humans. They often see this as aggressive play that needs to be interrupted. You must always look at the dogs that are involved and what the rest of their body is

telling you. The dog that is on the bottom is often times the one that is in charge of the game and controls when the game begins and when it ends.

2. **Chasing:** Multiple dogs will often be involved in this game. This is a great game, but must be supervised well. Small dogs may get injured by big dogs who are not watching where they are going. Occasionally, you will also notice one or more dogs trying to calm the game by using the split-up technique. The dog being chased is the dog in charge and in control.

3. **Tug:** This is a great game between two dogs who are not competing for a position in the pack. If it is a game for fun, you will see relaxed bodies from both dogs and when one lets go, the other will tease the dog with the toy to initiate play again. A third dog that is trying to split up the behavior to avoid potential conflict will sometimes interrupt this game. When a third dog attempts to play tug with the two, conflict may arise. Tug is something that should never be done between a human and a dog when there are multiple dogs around.

4. **Boxing:** This game is normally played by two dogs that stand on their back legs and "box" with each other. This

game may also be interrupted by a third dog attempting to split up the behavior.

Mounting

Though this behavior seems inappropriate and embarrassing to humans, it is very normal and natural for dogs. Interruption is on a per-case basis.

All dogs, regardless of sex or alteration may mount. There are **three different types of mounting**.

1. **Arousal:** This occurs when a dog becomes too excited. Mounting is very brief and has little meaning. Mounting will usually occur on the backside or flank area. There is no need to interrupt this behavior, as it will dissipate quickly. The dog mounting is never "pushy" towards the other dog. However, this mounting behavior can turn into sexual mounting.

2. **Sexual:** This is a natural behavior that dogs do regardless of sex or alteration. A dog can be "pushy" when doing this and will sometimes disregard any signals coming from the dog he is mounting. This is when the dog has become "fixated" and must be interrupted. Sexual mounting will be more precise on the backside or on the flank by young puppies. You

will see a penis extension and possibly swelling. Humping can continue after dog has dismounted. This behavior can also turn into dominant mounting.

3. **Dominant:** This mounting can occur at any time. It can be very "pushy" and can become aggressive if the mounted dog does not submit. However, I do not interrupt this play unless you see the dominant dog taking advantage of the submissive dog or if the mounted dog becomes aggressive. This can turn into sexual once dominance has been established.

Inappropriate Behavior

There are many inappropriate behaviors that should not be allowed in daycare. By being conscientious of these behaviors, you can interrupt them before they cause altercations.

A dog **disrespecting other dogs' signals** is the most common inappropriate behavior you will run into. This may be a dog that wants to play and is not backing off a dog that does not want to play. I always allow a couple of minutes before interrupting to give the dogs a chance to work it out themselves. You can interrupt this behavior with a verbal ("that's enough") and/or by using the split-up technique. If a dog becomes a bully, or is fixated on a particular dog, you may have to implement a time-out.

Resource guarding can be a problem that needs to be interrupted immediately. Dogs need to understand that all things belong to you, and their role is not to guard that resource. Dog may resource guard the supervisor, pool, toys, space, other dogs or the water bowl.

Excessively rough play can initiate altercations. If both dogs are being equal participants, do not interrupt, however, if one dog is being too rough and lacks self-control, you may have to interrupt. There is a good chance that the dog will not slow down long enough to read any signals that may be given to him by his playmate.

Uninvited play occurs when a dog approaches two or more dogs who are playing. He will attempt to become part of the play. If the group of dogs playing allows him to join, there is nothing for you to do. However, if they spend time ignoring him or pause play due to his presence, you will need to interrupt. Allow the dog to read and respond the group's signals before interrupting.

Excessive mounting is an inappropriate behavior if the dog becomes fixated or becomes pushy or aggressive.

Tagging is a behavior that can be mixed with rough or uninvited play. Tagging occurs when a dog uses his mouth to "tag" a dog on the back of the neck. Sometimes tagging can occur on other parts of the body. This behavior should be interrupted immediately.

Fixation can occur with play or mounting. This behavior exists when a dog is disrespecting signals of another dog, and will not leave the dog alone. This behavior will need to be interrupted immediately. Typically this behavior must be interrupted with a time-out.

Indirect Aggression is the most serious inappropriate behavior as it can cause harm to you or other dogs. Indirect aggression occurs when a dog gets excited about something but is unable to obtain it. In order to release his frustration over not getting the item he wants, he may release this energy on a nearby human or dog by attacking it. For example, a dog that is not allowed to have a tennis ball may get frustrated and attack something else like you or another dog. A dog may also get too excited when other dogs are jumping on a human or barking at another dog through a fence and it results in indirect aggression. Be very aware of the dogs that you have in the group and which ones may reach that excited state too quickly, get frustrated and lash out. Indirect aggression is a real problem that can occur so quickly that it usually ends up in a fight.

Interrupting Inappropriate Behavior

When supervising daycare you want to do the least amount of work as possible, as you want dogs to work conflict out themselves. In the beginning, you may have to be more involved, but once you have established your leadership you will find that there will be less work for you, especially as you begin to have a regular play group. You will find there are certain dogs in your regular group who will actually help you interrupt inappropriate behavior and will be instrumental in teaching other dogs appropriate behavior. Just make sure these dogs do not become "hall monitors" who interrupt play prematurely.

When interrupting inappropriate behavior, you will first give a verbal. This verbal will be the name of the dog followed by "that's enough." Stay calm and matter-of-fact when giving this command. If a new dog does not understand what this command means, you will give the command while using the split-up technique. [1] Be sure to stay consistent until the dog redirects himself from the dog or object. For example, if a dog is mounting another dog inappropriately and is disrespecting another dog's signals, start by giving a verbal "that's enough." If the dog does not know what this means, or is fixated on the other dog, you will physically position yourself between the two dogs. Face the dog who is being disrespectful, and begin to walk towards him. Do this without touching the dog. Continue to do this until he redirects himself by walking away. If I have to do three split-ups in a row, I go to the next level, which is time-out on leash. I put the dog on leash and make him stand beside me for at least one minute before being allowed free again. If I have to do the on-leash time-out three times, he goes into a crate or x-pen for a time-out. This time-out is also about one minute. If I have to do the crate or x-pen time-out three times, he goes inside for the remainder of the play session. If you have a very large play group, you may need to utilize a crate time-out rather than using the on-leash time-out.

---

[1] See pages 19 and 28 for more information on this technique.

The purpose of the interruption is to communicate to the dog that inappropriate behavior means attention and playtime will end. Having good timing when giving verbal warnings or time-outs is crucial so you can communicate to the dog exactly which action they did that is not acceptable. Be patient and be consistent as it may take multiple tries to communicate which behaviors are inappropriate.

3. Altercations

Altercations and disagreements occur during interaction and cannot be completely avoided. Understand that this is a risk that all daycares must take into consideration, but that most altercations can be avoided. Dogs have altercations for various reasons. It can be that a dog is tired or grumpy, is being disrespectful of another dog's signals, or it could be that two dogs just do not get along. Understanding communication and interaction.

Not every altercation is going to cause harm nor is it going to need to be interrupted. Each altercation will be different based on the dogs involved and what precipitated prior to the altercation. There are three different types of altercations:

1. **Accidental:** A dog may get too rough or excited during play causing another dog to yelp, whine or cry. This is typically over very quickly. Think about the last time you played Twister or any similar, physical game. If someone accidentally steps on your foot, you may wince or yell out,

but you are likely to forgive quickly and resume play. Dogs react in this same way, and will resume play after a shake off.

2. **Warning:** This occurs when a dog is being too rough during play because of a lack of control. This may cause the irritated dog to bark, growl or snap. This will sound like a fight but is usually very quick lived and dissipates quickly. Dogs may separate themselves and find other playmates for a period. You will only need to interrupt if the dog lacking self-control continues to play too rough, and does not respect the dog who has used Level 2 signals.

3. **Fight:** There are various reasons why fights occur. Usually a fight will sound worse than it really is. Dogs will usually fight in a boxing or wrestling fashion. Sometimes they will end without your interruption, but if interruption is needed, use an air horn to distract the dogs. Do not put your body between two or more dogs who are fighting.

Interrupting a Fight

There may be times to when it is impossible to prevent a fight from occurring. Knowing how to calmly and confidently break up a fight will increase the chances of everyone remaining safe and injury free.

As a leader, you must remain calm, confident and matter-of-fact. You should never let your emotions show, even if you are nervous.

The first step will be a verbal ("that's enough"). Use the same tone you would use when interrupting inappropriate behavior. You may have to raise your volume but only if the dogs are being loud themselves. If the verbal does not work you will need to separate the dogs. This must be done carefully so you do not become injured as the result of indirect aggression from either dog.

If you have one initiator and one receiver then you should be able to grab the back legs or under the haunches of the initiator. Gently pull him backwards and move him sideways so he loses balance and becomes distracted. Do this slowly and gently so the dog cannot rip the skin of the other dog. If both dogs are initiating the fight, then two people should be available to separate the dogs. Physically separating the dogs should be done after the verbal and air horn have been tried. Do not use any adversives such as a water hose or objects that could cause physical harm to the dogs such as hitting or whipping. After the dogs are separated, put them in a time-out in order to allow them to calm down.

Chapter 5
Understanding Dog Personality

When supervising or evaluating dogs for daycare, it is important that you understand what makes up a dog's personality so you can properly evaluate him. A dog's personality is made up of six different attributes. You can attempt to modify a dog's personality by improving on each individual attribute, though there are some dogs who cannot be modified due to hereditary problems.

1. Temperament: This is the "attitude" the dog is born with. Most temperaments can be modified through proper training. Knowing a dog's temperament will also give you a good idea as to what type of player he may be.

1. **Dominant-** A dog with a dominant temperament is a natural leader. This dog will control a situation if allowed to do so. If this dog is challenged for the leadership role by a weaker, non-consistent pack member, he may become difficult to deal with. It is important that this dog has a consistent leader (you). Dominant dogs are not always aggressive, just more forceful. These dogs are similar to natural born leaders within the human race.

2. **Submissive-** A submissive dog submits to a leader with little argument. He is comfortable in the role he has been placed in

within the pack, and does not mind being a follower. If the pack leader is inconsistent, he may attempt to take over, however, this often stresses the dog out until leadership from a human has been established. Dogs in this case can become nervous and lose confidence if no leader is present in the home.

3. **Fearful-** A fearful dog consistently has phobias such as being afraid of strangers, thunderstorms, new places, going for a ride, being left alone, meeting new dogs, etc. He has a hard time adjusting to new, different and stressful situations. This dog will often flee from scary situations. If he is unable to flee, he may resort to Level II signals quickly, and may be deemed a "fear biter." This issue can be more problematic than dealing with a truly vicious dog in that this dog is often unpredictable. Confidence building exercises will help this dog learn to deal with fearful situations without resorting to fleeing or biting.

4. **Nervous-** A nervous dog has a hard time adjusting to new, different and stressful situations. He will often look to his owner for reassurance. He will more than likely not flee or snap but instead tries to hide behind objects or owner.

5. **Aggressive-** In this context, "aggressive" does not mean "forceful," it means "vicious." This dog is quick to snap or

bite without warning, and will not back down. These dogs are difficult to work with and are often a danger to other dogs and people. Vicious dogs are usually born with this "seed." Occasionally this behavior can be modified when the dog is a puppy, but typically there is nothing that can be done to change this temperament. These dogs are often euthanized as they are a danger to society. Only a trained professional, knowledgeable in dog behavior, can appropriately deem a dog as aggressive or vicious. There are often times underlying issues that explain the behavior of the dog. Fear aggression is often times misunderstood for aggression.

6. **Indifferent**: This is a dog who care nothing about what is going on around him. This is an unusual temperament for dogs because they are pack animals.

7. **Flexible**: This dog has an excellent temperament, as he is able to adjust quickly to new environments, people or dogs. He can be dominant or submissive depending on the situation, and does not mind being the leader or follower. He is aware of what is going on around him, and does well with controlling himself. Unfortunately, this is a rare temperament in dogs today, however, it is possible to assist dogs in becoming flexible through proper training and socialization.

General Recommendations: If dog is fearful or nervous, daycare is a great place for him to be. He needs to learn how to be a dog so he can learn how to deal with the stressors he may encounter. He needs daycare more than any other dog no matter his age or size. It is important that as a supervisor you help the dog learn how to be a dog by building his confidence and by assisting with his communication skills. Do not baby, coddle or reassure a fearful or nervous dog as this will reinforce the issue.

2. Play Type: A dog's playing ability

1. **Player A:** This dog loves to play with anything and anyone. He understands how to play with dogs. He knows when to be submissive and when to be dominant during play. This dog is a great candidate for day care.

2. **Player B:** This dog is submissive and only enjoys playing with dogs that are similar. This dog is unsure how to handle dominant dogs and chooses not to play with them. This dog is great for daycare. As a supervisor, you will help build his confidence and skills so he is comfortable playing with all types of dogs.

3. **Player C:** This dog is dominant, also known as a "bully." He plays well but tends to push his weight around. Often times if another dog challenges him, he will back down and show

submissiveness. On occasion, a dog may continue to push his weight around possibly cause a problem. He is fine for daycare. As a supervisor, you can help this dog learn that being a bully does not work by interrupting inappropriate behaviors.

4. **Player D:** This dog is very nervous and does not understand how to play with other dogs. He will benefit a lot from daycare, as is important he learns how to play. This dog is not to be coddled or soothed.

5. **Player E:** This dog is extremely fearful. Before labeling a dog an E Player, they must try day care on several occasions. If a dog continues to be an E Player it means he is too nervous for daycare and is unable to function around other dogs. He is constantly trying to escape and never relaxes. Outside training needs to take place before re-testing. This dog should never be eliminated from daycare for the long term.

6. **Player F:** This dog attacks other dogs for no reason and is not a good candidate for daycare until outside training has taken place.

General Recommendations: Player D needs to continue to attend on a regular basis. It is important that a Player E dog gets some training and attempts daycare again. It is not good to leave the dog out of daycare as interaction will help him learn to be a more confident dog. Doing this may cause other behavior problems to occur.

3. Dog Language Skill: This is the dog's ability to communicate effectively with other dogs and people. This will be linked directly with a dog's confidence level.

1. **Excellent**- This dog knows how to communicate effectively with other dogs. Does very well at calming situations down.

2. **Good**-This dog knows the basics of dog language. He does well with other dogs that know dog language but does not know how to communicate with dogs that are not good with dog language.

3. **Fair**- This dog knows a few dog language skills but does not know the appropriate time to use them. When dog uses a signal, he does not give the receiver enough time to respond before moving to a higher, more aggressive level of communication.

4. **Poor:** This dog has no knowledge of dog language skills. This is unable to communicate effectively during stressful situations.

General Recommendations: Dogs that are not good with dog language need daycare. Be sure that these dogs are allowed to play with dogs that possess excellent and good dog language skills. Dogs with poor skills should not be left out of daycare, but should attend daycare on a more regular basis.

4. Social skills: This will help you determine how well a dog is socialized with people and dogs. This will give you a good idea on how to deal with this dog on a regular basis when in day care.

1. **Excellent:** This dog loves people and does not hesitate to have everyone pet him. He enjoys being around other dogs.

2. **Good:** This dog likes most people, but may be a little weary of people who are not dog lovers or who are noticeably afraid of dogs. He does well with dogs who are friendly but may not do well with dogs who are nervous or afraid.

3. **Fair:** This dog only likes people and dogs he is familiar with. He takes a while to warm up to new people and dogs.

4. **Poor:** This is not social with people or dogs except for his own pack.

General Recommendations: If you have a dog that is Fair or Poor, you need to be sure to use good dog language skills to help him feel as comfortable as he can. Do not force this dog to be petted and do not try to encourage the dog to come up to you. Allow the dog to come to you when he is ready.

5. Confidence: Confidence affects most areas of a dog's life and personality. A dog with low confidence will have a nervous or fearful temperament and will most likely be a Player D or E. A dog with confidence issues will have trouble problem solving and will not have great dog language skills.

1. **High:** This dog is able to handle different and stressful situations without a problem. He is not afraid to try or learn ncw things.

2. **Moderate:** This dog is able to handle different and stressful situations with a minimal amount of nervousness or stress. Dog has to be coaxed into trying or learning something new when out of his comfort zone. You will not see any problems from him when he is in his comfort zone.

3. **Low-** This dog has a hard time dealing with new, different and stressful situations. Dog must be coaxed to try or learn something new and even then, may still shut down. He will show small amounts of stress or nervousness even when in his comfort zone.

4. **None**: This dog is completely unable to handle new, different or stressful situations. He is nervous and stressed even in his comfort zone or home. He is unable to be coaxed to try or learn something new until confidence begins to build.

General Recommendations: Do not baby or coddle a dog if he has confidence issues. Always stay positive and refrain from ever using any type of corrections. Dogs with high to low confidence need to be in daycare on a regular basis. If a dog has no confidence, he needs some professional training to help build his confidence before returning to day care.

6. Problem Solving Skill: A dog must be able to problem-solve in order to deal with conflicting situations. This is the hardest attribute to see naturally without doing some training exercises. This is not an attribute that you have to know in order to accurately determine a dog's true personality.

1. **Excellent**: This dog can take any situation and have the final outcome rule in their favor.

2. **Good**: This dog is good at problem solving during familiar situations, but struggles during new situations.

3. **Poor**: This dog has no ability to problem-solve in any situation. Has never been taught to use his brain.

Chapter 6
Standard Operating Procedures

Every business has standard operating procedures used to create consistency regarding its processes. As the daycare supervisor, you may be asked to input your ideas into the creation of new standard operating procedures related to the daycare portion of the business.

Intake

This process details what should be done when dogs are dropped off at daycare. Your front desk staff should be aware of all requirements for daycare dogs, which include a specific daycare waiver form and a behavior questionnaire. Dogs should then be taken to their own kennels (these will be used later for naptime).

Dogs often come with a collar and leash, so decide if you will keep those with the dog or send them home with the owner. If you choose to keep them, always keep them where dogs do not have access to them, as they may become damaged.

Kennel/Crate Cards

It is crucial that you have information on each dog that comes into the facility. Each kennel or crate card should list the dog's name, breed and color, as well as the owner and veterinarian names and contact information. Also list the identifying kennel or crate number on the card, and any pertinent information pertaining to daycare restrictions, such as which dogs he can or cannot be with, or any health issues you know about.

Daycare Collars

I do not recommend you allow dogs to play while wearing their own collars. The collars can get damaged or can cause harm during play through choking. Your facility may choose to purchase or have clients purchase breakaway collars which will come off easily if a dog gets caught on something, or if the collar is stuck in another dog's mouth. The issue with these collars is that if the collar is lost, there is no identification on the dog. This becomes problematic in the unfortunate event that a dog escapes from a play area, or if you have multiple dogs in a play group that look similar. You can purchase these collars with identification on them (such as kennel number and facility phone number), however, they are expensive, and again, not helpful if the collar is lost.

I recommend tab collars. These are inexpensive and can be sized appropriately for every dog. They also can have identifying information written on them, and can be thrown away after each visit. I typically direct facilities to TabBand.com. These collars will still break away if need be. They also can be easily replaced if damaged during play. Buying these collars in different colors will also help with the identification process. I use white collars to identify dogs who have been evaluated in the past, and who can be put in a play group with any dog. Yellow means that the dog needs an evaluation. Red collars denote dogs who have special restrictions, or require additional resources during daycare. For instance, you may have one "red collar" dog who you have deemed during evaluation to be intolerant of male dogs, and another that absolutely cannot be in a play group with small dogs. It is possible that a dog starts out in your daycare as a red collar dog, but graduates to a white collar dog through additional training. It is imperative that this information is written on the kennel or crate card in order to keep the play groups safe.

Bringing Dogs into Play Area

It is important dogs work for the opportunity to go into the play area in order to teach them self-control and problem-solving skills, and to establish yourself as the leader of the group.

When you approach a dog in his kennel or run, ensure he is exhibiting appropriate behavior by not jumping, barking or whining. If any of these is displayed, ignore him and do not take him from his kennel or crate. Once he is exhibiting appropriate behavior for at least three seconds, you may approach. When you enter the kennel, ignore the dog if he begins jumping. This means you will not look at, touch or talk to him. When he has "four-on-the-floor" for three seconds, attempt to put the leash on. Always approach and stand to the dog's side, and do not lean toward the dog's face while leashing, as this is seen as confrontational. By approaching and standing to the side of the dog, you are using the same appropriate approach technique used during dog-dog interaction.

Do not allow the dog to run through the kennel or any other

door without permission. Control each threshold the dog crosses. He does not have to sit, and you do not have to exit the door first to establish your leadership, he just has to wait for your permission. You want to teach self-control and problem-solving skills, not obedience or that you are dominant. To do this exercise, keep the leash loose and begin opening the door. If the dog moves forward, close the door immediately. Once the dog is relaxed and not pulling forward, begin opening the door again. If the dog is good while the door is open, give him the permission word ("okay") and go through the door.

To teach self-control while walking, use the "object of desire" exercise. In this case, the object of desire is the play area. Use a short leash and appropriate leash handling skills.[2] Keep your thumb tucked in your pocket or belt loop so you keep your arm at your side, and so you are not tempted to pull back on or correct the dog by "popping" the leash. Walk forward if the dog is not pulling on the leash. If he begins to pull, walk backwards until he is walking with you. At this point, you can move forward again until he pulls. During this exercise you are never stationary. The reward for the dog is getting to be closer to the object he desires (play area), while the consequence is having it taken away with distance. You can also use this exercise when the dog is approaching other dogs on leash or people. If you have to back up repeatedly, put the dog in a thirty second time out, then bring him out to try again. Once he is close to the gate, give him an audible "okay" and allow him to approach.

---

[2] Visit our YouTube channel to see this exercise

When at the gate require the dog to show self-control before giving permission to enter. These same exercises should be done anytime the dog enters or exits the play area.

Nap Time

Much like humans, dogs need rest to avoid becoming "grumpy." Nap time in the middle of the day is crucial to ensure that play stays safe as some altercations occur because dogs are just tired of playing and interacting with one another. Nap time should be a separate from the play area. The dogs should have their own areas such as a kennel or crate. This two hour break will not only allow the dogs to have much needed rest, but will also allow daycare staff to have lunch, switch shifts and clean up before the afternoon session begins.

Attendance

While it is important that dogs attend daycare regularly to improve their dog communication skills, they must also have time to develop their socialization with humans. Many times, behavioral issues can occur if dogs attend daycare too often. I recommend dogs attend daycare no more than three times per week. If you notice a dog comes more than three days, talk to the owner about possible cutting back, or, if this is not possible, inquire if you can use the other days to work on human interaction with the staff. A break from daycare will also ensure dogs get plenty of mental and physical rest between visits. Again, dogs who are rested are less likely to be involved in altercations and disagreements.

Staff to Dog Ratio

I am frequently asked how many dogs a supervisor should oversee at any given time. This number will vary based on your experience and the group of dogs you have. Some days, you may only be able to have a play group of five if you have difficult dogs, while other days you may have a group of twenty regulars who have adjusted to one another's personalities. Your comfort level will increase as you gain more experience working with dogs.

Cleaning Procedures

Your facility may have cleaning procedures already in its SOPs. Cleaning procedures should be based on your play areas flooring to ensure it is disinfected properly. Be sure your SOPs indicate who is responsible for cleanup each day. This will depend on your hours, staffing and services offered. In order to keep your play areas and kennels safe, it is vital they are cleaned daily.

Preparing Your Play Area

Regardless if your play area is indoors or outdoors, there are certain steps to take to prepare the area before dogs are brought out for the day. This will be a part of your normal routine.

First check all fencing in the area. This is especially important if you are outside. Ensure that there are no weak spots or holes in or under the fencing, and that no sharp edges are along or on the fencing. Also check all gates to ensure they close and lock properly. Your gate system should be a double gate to increase security.

Next, make sure your play area is clean. Typically this is done the night before after all daycare participants have been checked out, however, it is always a good idea to double check. Sanitation of play areas is key to prevent illnesses from being passed to daycare attendees. As you are checking for cleanliness, check for any holes that dogs may have dug. This will help to eliminate injury from dogs tripping in holes while running.

Once you know your area is safe, you can begin setup for daycare.

Set-up for Daycare

A well-stocked daycare should have the following items:

1. A clean water bucket with fresh water. Depending on the size of your group you may need two buckets. You will also need a way to refill your bucket(s). This may mean you need to pull a hose into the area or fill up extra jugs of water. Be sure to fill up your pool if you are using one. Once the water is taken care of you can bring out any toys you will be using during playtime.

2. A time-out zone. If this is a crate, ensure the crate is clean and functioning properly. If you have a fenced off area for your time-outs, ensure that the fencing is secure. I do not recommend utilizing a fenced-in area for time outs unless it is not see-through (i.e. chain link), as barrier aggression can occur.

3. For personal use during supervision you will also need your daycare attendance list, extra collars, writing utensils, leashes,

two-way radios[3] and an air horn. These items are non-negotiable.

Morning Routine

When dogs arrive for the day, they should be placed into a run or secure crate. This will allow you to prepare the play areas and do physicals before daycare begins.

Have an attendance sheet available at the beginning of each day. If you offer boarding, be sure you know which dogs will not be arriving through the door, but are already in the facility. The sheet should also show where each dog is, i.e. kennel number or crate, and if the dog is new and in need of an evaluation.

Walk through the facility and ensure that all dogs scheduled for daycare are in the appropriate location. I recommend checking each dog off and highlighting the dogs that need an evaluation. Knowing who you have in attendance will also help you accelerate the evaluation process. Evaluations and physicals should be done prior to bringing regular attendees out to the play areas.

Be sure to gather the items previously listed. You will also want to have the following readily available:

- Report cards and evaluation forms
- Poop Scoop and bucket
- Mop and bucket (if inside)

---

[3] A two-way radio may not be needed if your area is small and you have assistance within speaking distance.

When each dog enters the play area they should be checked off the list so each is accounted for. You will also use this list when it is time for dogs to go in for their naps. Always keep a list of dogs that come and go from the play area as small dogs can easily hide and get left outside.

Your two-way radio is crucial if your play area is away from other employees. You will use this to call for dogs to be brought to the play area or for assistance in the case of an altercation or injury. I recommend that you have an assistant each day that can help you bring dogs out and put them up at naptime. As the supervisor, you will never leave dogs unattended.

Never go into your play area without an air horn. If the air horn is older be sure it is working properly. Please check the air horn away from all dogs. The air horn will be used in the event of an altercation between dogs.

Chapter 7
Evaluating Dogs for Daycare

I cannot express enough the importance of properly evaluating dogs for daycare. The primary purpose of an evaluation is to learn about a dog's personality and temperament which will allow you to anticipate problems that could occur during daycare, and will also allow you to prevent altercations and decrease risks. An evaluation begins the moment you meet a dog. Take into consideration how the dog responds to your approach, to you entering his space and his responses to verbal words.

Behavior Questionnaire

Ensure you have an initial behavior questionnaire completed by the owner for each dog. You will use this questionnaire to guide you in the remainder of the evaluation process. This particular tool will give you some insight into what issues you may need to look out for later on. Keep in mind, this questionnaire may only be indicative of how a dog acts at home or around its owners, so do not base your evaluation solely on this.

Look over the questionnaire to determine what issues you may need to work on with a dog. If the questionnaire states that a dog is not good with small dogs, then test him with small dogs first. If the questionnaire states the dog is not good with male dogs, then you will want to test him with male dogs first. This will allow you to know if this is truly an issue, or if it is an issue only in a certain environment.

Be sure to watch a dog's body language and signals during this process to avoid possible altercations.

The questionnaire should be an easy to fill out form. Use multiple choice questions, and give owners spaces for additional comments. Below is a list of questions to include:

- Has your dog ever been to daycare before? If so, why does he no longer attend that particular daycare?
- Has your dog visited the dog park? How did he do?
- How does your dog do with small/large dogs?
- How does your dog do with male/female dogs?
- Has your dog had any formal training? If so, what type of training did he receive?
- What behavior problems does your dog have, if any?
- Does your dog have any health problems? If so, explain.
- How is your dog on leash around dogs/people? How is your dog off-leash around dogs/people?

Leave a section for owners to put their opinions and/or concerns.

Physical

The physical is an important part of the evaluation process. This will allow you to evaluate the dog's response to be handled, and will also allow you to check each dog for existing wounds or physical concerns prior to play. Note concerns on the dog's kennel card, or report card. If any existing wound needs attention, alert the owner before allowing the dog into the play yard for the day. This will prevent owners from feeling the wound occurred at your business, and will also allow you and the owner to work together to get the wound or problem area properly treated.

Specifically look for sores, scrapes, cuts, bruises, hair loss, lumps, bumps and sore areas. Use your hands in a massaging fashion to locate these. Take both hands and begin by rubbing down both sides of the dog. Be sure you are firm enough to feel lumps or bumps. Run both hands underneath the dog along the belly and chest. All four legs should be checked in the same fashion. Visually look underneath the dog and along the legs for any cuts or scrapes. You will also look in the ears, and at paws, pads and toenails. If a dog has long toenails they may need to be trimmed before daycare to prevent breaking or harm to other dogs. If you notice the pads on the dog are velvety soft, keep in mind that the pad could become irritated or tear during play depending on the material you use in your play area. Always use calming signals when approaching and during the physical. Try to squat during the physical instead of hovering over the dog in a confrontational way. The physical should only take a couple of minutes to perform, and should be done for each new dog coming to daycare or dogs that are not regular attendees. Many of the owners of regular attendees will learn to advise you of any wounds or issues when they check in.

Lone Evaluation

Evaluating new dogs without other dogs or owners in the area will allow you to determine the dog's personality. This will allow you to choose the appropriate dogs for the testing process.

Observe the dog as you take it from the kennel to the play area. Also observe how the dog reacts to walking on a leash and getting the leash on and off. If you walk past other dogs on the way to the play area, notice how the dog reacts. Use the "object of desire" exercise while walking to the play area, and do not allow a jumping dog out of a kennel until he has displayed self-control. Allow the dog to explore the play area alone and unleashed. Is he attempting to hide and cower in a corner, or is he actively exploring the area? This will give you insight into his confidence and temperament.

Once he seems comfortable in the yard, interact with him verbally and physically. Use his name to get his attention, pet him if he allows and attempt to engage him in play. It is important to know if he will respond to his name as you may use it frequently in daycare. This will also give you information regarding his social skills with people, and his excitement about toys or games.

The time it takes for the lone evaluation should take approximately five minutes. Once completed you will move on to testing with other dogs.

Multiple Dog Testing

This is the most difficult and important part of the evaluation process. The more you practice this step, the easier it will become.

Your goal in the multiple dog testing is to see how your testing dog will respond to dogs with different personalities, confidence levels, communication signals and social skills. Look for potential problems from the dog you are evaluating. Introduce dogs one at a time, and allow them to interact for a short period of time. Once you see how the dogs interact together you will decide the next personality type to test with. You will do this with a minimum of three dogs before allowing the remainder of the play group out. Use dogs that differ as much as possible in personality.

Let's look at some examples:

1. Imagine the dog you are testing appears to have a submissive temperament, low confidence, good communication skills, good social skills with people and fair problem-solving skills. There are many potential issues that could arise. The testing dog could respond inappropriately with other dogs by snapping, running, shaking, trembling or growling. This could occur quickly as distance increasing signals and not calming signals. For your first introduction, bring out a dog with excellent communication skills, good patience, moderate confidence and a possible Player A. You need a dog you trust that will respond appropriately to the testing dog's potential distance increasing signals. Also, a Player A dog will allow you to see if your testing dog is playful. Once the first dog is out and you see how the testing dog is going to respond to him, you will better know which type of personality to use for the next introduction. If the dog you

are evaluating does well with the first dog, bring out a dog that is not consistently respectful of signals, but is playful. This will allow you to know how the dog you are evaluating responds to a dog that may not have good self-control or patience. If the dog you are evaluating reacts inappropriately, it is okay. This gives you better information for which dog to introduce next. After the first two introductions, you now know the dog you are evaluating does well with dogs that have good signals and are confident. For the third introduction, bring out a dog as similar as possible to the dog you are evaluating. This will allow you to see if he can relax and adjust to the playgroup. You and the other dogs can then begin assisting your new dog with building its confidence and communication skills.

2.   The next dog you evaluate may have an outgoing personality and be full of confidence and playfulness, but not be great with communication skills or problem-solving skills. Though the dog is playful, you may potentially have a dog that could cause issues by not respecting signals given by dogs that are not as playful. In this case, your first dog to test with is one with excellent communication skills, moderate confidence, excellent problem-solving skills and but does not care to play. I expect this first dog to communicate to the dog I am testing that not every dog wants to play all the time. If the dog you are evaluating respects these signals, then the second dog to bring out should be one that has poor communication skills.

This will allow you to see if he will continue to be respectful of poor signals or if he will become a bully. His response to the second dog will determine the third dog you bring out. Do not bring out another overly playful dog as this will interrupt the evaluation process because these two dogs will more than likely play together, ignoring the rest of the group. This will not facilitate the learning process for the dog being evaluated, and will not allow him to build his communication skills and self-control.

3. If you have a medium-sized dog that the owners believe is aggressive towards smaller dogs, the first dog you introduce should be a smaller dog with excellent skills who will respond appropriately to the medium-sized dog if there should be an altercation. This will allow you to better understand if the issue is actually toward smaller dogs, or if there is an underlying issue with smaller dogs in the medium-sized dog's regular environment. This will also allow you to work with the owner to begin taking steps to correct negative associations with smaller dogs.

Again, keep in mind that the primary purpose of the evaluation is to identify and begin to work on potential issues that can arise in your playgroup.

Chapter 8
Setting Owners' Expectations

A supervisor's job does not end when the play groups are put away for the day. There are still many things that need to be completed. Besides ensuring the play area is properly sanitized, the supervisor will also be in charge of writing reports, evaluations, explaining behavior to clients and selling daycare. These are all part of customer service, and the main goal of customer service is to set a client's expectations.

Report Cards

Report cards should be completed for each dog that attends daycare. If you have a dog that comes three or more times a week, you can do one at the end of the week. Do not be afraid to write down honest comments in your reports. Sometimes dogs have bad days just as humans do. Be prepared to explain to the owner what occurred, and offer solutions for undesirable behavior. If a dog has improved because of daycare, be sure to relay that as well. It is important to personalize each report card. They do not have to include essays, but should give an owner honest feedback on how their dog is doing. Sometimes it is okay to just write "Thanks for bringing Fred this week! He is a great addition to our playgroup."

Helping Clients Understand Their Dog's Behavior

You do not have to be a trainer or behavior consultant to help clients understand their dog's behavior while in daycare. Here are some techniques to remember when speaking to owners about their dog's progress and/or behavior—especially if a dog has displayed unwanted behavior:

1.   Always have clear communication with owners. Be upfront and honest about their dog's behavior, even if their dog did not have a great day. Typically they will appreciate your honesty, and will appreciate your plan for assisting them with undesirable behavior going forward. Use plain English when talking with them and stay away from using technical terms. Use analogies if you can to help them understand better, or relate to them in another way (it is okay to tell them about the time your dog ate the couch, or got into a disagreement with another dog). Remember, you are not trying to impress them with your knowledge, and it is important to not be condescending.   If an owner seems extremely upset by their dog's behavior, especially if it is a behavior they have not seen before, give them reasons for why the behavior may have occurred, and again offer solutions. Always end on a positive note by relaying something their dog did well that day.

2.   Encourage owners to continue to bring their dogs to daycare, and assist with a plan for warding off bad behavior,

or for continuing to enhance good behavior at home. If you have access to informational handouts, use them. You can also refer them to a positive trainer/behavior consultant in your area—one who understands dog behavior and dog interaction.

3. Many times, it is not what you say, but how you say it that will determine if an owner will continue to use your facility or will follow-up with extra training. So be confident, honest, simple, empathetic and positive to help owners understand but feel good about their dog's behavior.

Selling Daycare

At many facilities, the first people clients meet and/or speak to are the receptionists. It is important that they understand why daycare is important, and know some basics about the programs your facility offers. They will be crucial to the selling process. In fact, any employee who interacts with clients will assist in promoting the program. Work with management or marketing to come up with a reward program or contest to see which employee can sign up the most daycare dogs. This will help build a little friendly competition, but will also motivate employees to learn more about the daycare process and its importance to dogs.

If your facility offers more than one service, i.e. boarding and grooming, put together packages that will help cross sell each service.

If you only offer daycare in your facility, but together packages that will influence clients to bring their dogs more often. For example, if your facility charges $25 per day per dog for daycare, offer a package of 10 days for a reduced rate of $200. You can also give multi-dog discounts. I recommend offering free evaluations to all daycare dogs. This way, owners will receive a report card detailing their dog's personality with personal recommendations and details about the benefits of daycare.

Provide a short handout to each client who leaves your boarding or grooming facility detailing the importance of daycare. Help clients understand that daycare can help ease the stresses of a boarding environment.

Improving Dog Behavior

One of your biggest roles as a daycare supervisor will be to improve the behavior and language skills of the dogs in your facility. This will assist in making your group as harmonious and safe as possible. As dogs' skills improve, so will their overall wellbeing. This in turn will result in loyal clients.

Teach your clients how to properly reward their dog at home, and how to interrupt or ignore unwanted behavior. Getting your clients involved with their dogs' education will also get them more engaged and interested in your business. It is important to build relationships with both the dogs and their owners in order to keep your business successful. Work on a plan together to improve dogs' communication skills and behavior.

Chapter 9
Excelling As a Dog Daycare Supervisor

I cannot express how important it is to practice your new skills! If you do not have a position as a daycare supervisor, there are other ways to put your knowledge to use.

Volunteering for a rescue or shelter group will not only allow you to practice your skills, but will also benefit the dogs as well. You will be able to provide valuable insight into a dog's personality and needs which will increase its chances of getting adopted to the right home.

If you are unable to locate a rescue or shelter group, visit the dog park on a regular basis. Do this without taking your own dog. Focus on dog interaction and problem-solve as if you were supervising a daycare. What behavior would you interrupt? How quickly can you evaluate a dog you do not know just by watching it interact?

There are many ways to gain experience. As long as you keep your mind open and continue learning you will be successful as a dog daycare supervisor. You will spend a career truly changing dogs for the better.

Chapter 10
Resources

Website: For the latest DogSpeak news, and to see how Nikki can help your daycare, visit www.dogspeak101.com

E-Training for Dogs: Bring Nikki's seminars, including "When Love Isn't Enough," to your home! www.e-trainingfordogs.com

Facebook: Get the latest news from DogSpeak!
www.facebook.com/DogSpeak101

YouTube: Check out exclusive training videos!
www.youtube.com/DogSpeak102

Other guides and books are available at Amazon.com

For examples of daycare report cards and evaluation reports please contact us at info@dogspeak101.com

ABOUT THE AUTHOR

Nikki Ivey, professional Dog Trainer/Behavior Consultant is the owner and founder of DogSpeak™. She has been working with dogs and their owners since 1996. She has spread her wealth of knowledge to not only the general public but to the professional pet world as well. She loves to educate individually and in groups, wanting all pet owners and professionals to have a better understanding of dogs and to have the healthiest possible relationship with them.

Nikki has spent many years learning to truly understand the nature of dogs and their motivations. By letting go of the "dominant pack theory" method, she is allowed to be more in tune with dogs, and more effective using her own method of training known as DogSpeak™. Nikki uses positive methods with negative punishment such as time-outs, stopping playtime and taking away attention. She doesn't use any form of physical correction such as correction collars, shock devices or fake bites. This allows dogs to show their true personality, builds their confidence and always leaves them happy. It also ensures that children aren't being taught to be negative or physical with their dogs when teaching.

Nikki believes in clearly communicating with dogs, setting their expectations and giving them a confident leader. She teaches foundation skills to dogs such as self-control and problem solving. Once a solid foundation is in place, you can begin to build the walls of real life manners that go beyond the traditional obedience training of sit, stay, down, come and heel. With real life manners your dog will know how to respond in situations without having to be commanded by you; however, when you do need to command your dog, they respond quickly and enthusiastically.

Nikki also owned and operated the first dog daycare in Tennessee and has spent the last seven years helping others build their successful daycares, either from the ground up or as an additive to an existing business. She trains staff members on dog behavior and interaction at daycares, veterinary clinics, and boarding facilities. Local rescue groups and shelters have started taking advantage of the knowledge and skill that Nikki has to help their foster parents understand the importance of foundation skills and being a confident, consistent leader.

In 2001, Nikki founded Tennessee Emergency Rescue and Recovery Association (TERRA), which uses K9s to locate missing persons and deceased individuals in water or land. She's not only a handler of a Human Remains Detection dog but also teaches other handlers to work their dog in HRD.

In addition to teaching, Nikki has also authored articles for various magazines and newspapers. She is a handler for KlaasKids, Inc. and the National Center for Missing and Exploited Children, and is a case manager for Polly Center.

In her spare time Nikki enjoys writing, and often incorporates her knowledge of search and rescue. Nikki's first novel, *Callout*, is available online at any large bookstore.

6119393R00047

Printed in Great Britain
by Amazon.co.uk, Ltd.,
Marston Gate.